THE BIBLE IN
SEVEN
PASSAGES

MIKE MAZZALONGO

BibleTalk.tv

Copyright © 2019 by Mike Mazzalongo

ISBN: 978-1-945778-84-1

BibleTalk Books
14998 E. Reno
Choctaw, Oklahoma 73020

Scripture quotations taken from the New American Standard Bible®, Copyright © 1960, 1962, 1963, 1968, 1971, 1972, 1973, 1975, 1977, 1995 by The Lockman Foundation Used by permission. (www.Lockman.org)

TABLE OF CONTENTS

INTRODUCTION	5
PASSAGE #1 *PRELUDE TO THE PROMISE*	11
PASSAGE #2 *GOD'S PROMISE TO FALLEN MAN*	19
PASSAGE #3 *THE PERSON OF PROMISE - HISTORICAL*	41
PASSAGE #4 *THE PERSON OF PROMISE - SPIRITUAL*	47
PASSAGE #5 *THE PROMISE REVEALED*	55
PASSAGE #6 *THE PROMISE REALIZED*	65
PASSAGE #7 *THE PROMISE FULFILLED*	77

ELEMENTARY SCHOOL
EVOLUTION

# GOVERNMENT
EVOLUTION = SCIENCE

# BIG TECH
SCIENCE = EVOLUTION / CLIMATE

MSM
EVOLUTION
CLIMATE
HUMANISM
SOCIALISM
} AS ACCEPTED NORMAL REALITY

HOLLYWOOD
EVOLUTION
CLIMATE
HUMANISM
} AS ENTERTAINMENT

ACADEMIA
EVOLUTION
CLIMATE
HUMANISM
SOCIALISM
} CREDIBILITY & ACCEPTANCE TO INDOCTRINATE THE NEXT GENERATION

INTRODUCTION

I want you to imagine a world where the Bible, as we know it, has been taken away. It is, perhaps, the year 2050 AD.

The Government, Big Tech, in league with academia, the news media and Hollywood have entered into a devil's scheme to undermine the veracity and limit access to the Bible as well as shame and condemn those who believe and use the Bible as their spiritual and moral guide for life in this world.

2050 AD

BIGOV
4 THE PEOPLE

spacebook

IVVY UNIVERSITY

ENN
EVERYWHERE
NEWS NETWORK

HOLLYMARK
ENTERTAINMENT AT YOUR FINGERTIPS

This has been achieved gradually as successive governments drifted to extreme positions setting up leaders who completely embraced policies and agendas that were devoid of any Christian principles. These were aided and abetted by Big Tech and academia who helped formulate, establish and disseminate a new narrative about life and death where God was not considered or even mentioned.

This was relatively easy to do because references concerning God or the use of the Bible were removed from the process of government and as a topic of study by academics decades before.

Once this new life narrative had been set by the primary education and government complex, it was an easy matter for this groupthink to be unilaterally affirmed by Big Tech and obtain message repetition by the news media (for the serious manner of repeating the propaganda) and propagation by the entertainment industry who dressed up the lie so it could be swallowed whole as diversion or emotional comfort. This scenario was neatly rounded out by the peddling of the lie to the successive generations through a corrupted university system.

Now, imagine 30 years of this taking place and arriving at a period in time when interplanetary travel is common, and all communication is digital because there are no more paper books being produced (a great victory for extreme environmentalists).

Oh, there may be some kooks who have stashed books in their attics and there are rumors of hidden bunkers containing thousands of original copies – but printed material is all created, processed, stored and transferred from Quantum Memory Storage Units located in strategic areas of the nation. It is from here that digital information is distributed to a chip embedded in each citizen's brain which is capable of displaying information that the eye sees as a hologram and the ear can detect as sound so that most entertainment, news and distance communication are transferred in this way.

One curious thing, however, in all this wizardly communication, no Bible is archived in the QMSU. This is because it was deemed fanatic and dangerous to the well-being of society and purged along with other controversial material and hate speech. In this regard, the embedded chips were programmed in such a way that they would not receive, transfer or store any material taken from the Bible.

DIGITAL INFORMATION

100101100
100110110
100011001
001011010
011010101
001001000
010101010

QUANTUM MEMORY STORAGE UNITS

NO BIBLE

RECEIVE
TRANSFER
VIEW
STORE

DATA CHIP

This would be a close version of the utopian and godless world dreamed of in John Lennon's (singer/song writer with the 20th century band, The Beatles) famous song entitled, "Imagine."

IMAGINE
JOHN LENNON

Imagine there's no heaven
It's easy if you try
No hell below us
Above us only sky

Imagine all the people
Living for today

Imagine there's no countries
It isn't hard to do
Nothing to kill or die for
And no religion, too

Imagine all the people
Living life in peace

You may say that I'm a dreamer
But I'm not the only one
I hope someday you'll join us
And the world will be as one

Imagine no possessions
I wonder if you can
No need for greed or hunger
A brotherhood of man

Imagine all the people
Sharing all the world

You may say that I'm a dreamer
But I'm not the only one
I hope someday you'll join us
And the world will live as one

In his lyrics, Lennon posits the idea that a peaceful, united, prosperous global community of mankind will only be possible if society removes the idea of God and the practice of religion. His implicit suggestion is that belief in God (and by extension the sustainment of religion by the single greatest resource of religion – which is the Bible) should be eliminated.

The logic is simple:
no God, no war... no Bible, no God and thus no war.

Imagine living in a world like the one I have just described? A world of dazzling communication technology but one that has successfully managed to suppress the access to and spread of God's printed Word! In such a world, believers would need to carry with them the essential message of the Bible in an extremely abbreviated format (that is, simple human memory) since, as I mentioned before, the embedded DATA CHIPS would not accept or retain Bible verses.

Of course, the average person would have great difficulty memorizing or accurately remembering the contents of one Bible book (in an attempt to create and maintain faith) let alone memorizing all 66 books that make up the Old and New Testament parts of the Bible. Perhaps 66 books were impossible to memorize, but what about seven? Not seven books but seven passages? Could we find seven passages that encapsulated all 66 books of the Bible?

Seven passages that, if memorized and remembered, would keep the essential message of God's Word intact in one's mind and heart. Seven passages that could explain God's overall plan of salvation, accurately identify Jesus and provide a lost sinner the good news by which his sins would be forgiven and his future glory revealed. Could all of this be done with only seven passages of Scripture?

The futuristic scenario that I have just described is a little far-fetched, even though we can see how some of these things might threaten us given what is going on in our society today. Who knows? Future generations of believers may have to struggle with similar issues in the decades to come. In the meantime, allow me to use this imagined introduction to establish the basis for a brief study entitled, "The Bible in Seven Passages."

If, for any reason, we had to memorize key passages in order to keep the overall message of the Bible alive in our minds, these are the seven passages I would recommend and why.

PASSAGE #1
GENESIS 1:1
PRELUDE TO THE PROMISE

> In the beginning God created the heavens and the earth.
> - Genesis 1:1

If Genesis is the foundational book of the Bible, then verse 1 of Genesis is the foundational verse of Genesis. The Bible is the most produced book in history, the most read book in history, therefore verse 1, where most people begin to read even if they do not finish, is the most read verse in the Bible, in history, in the world.

Henry Morris, in *The Genesis Record (page 37)*, says,

> ...if a person really believes Genesis 1:1, he will not find it difficult to believe anything else recorded in the Bible.

This verse does not try to prove the existence of God, it merely assumes it. Of course, it was written before any disbelief occurred, before any false system of belief to reject God was developed so it does not attempt to prove a self-evident fact.

However, this verse does contain the information necessary to refute all of man's subsequent false ideas about God and the creation. It is as if God knew what man (fallen because of sin) would ultimately think up to deny God and so in the very first verse of His message to mankind God preempts any possible false ideas about Himself.

7 Main Philosophies Refuted by Genesis 1:1

1. **Atheism** says there is no God.

    - Genesis 1:1 says that God created the heavens and the earth.

2. **Pantheism** says that everything is God. The trees, rivers, stars, etc. Pantheism is a form of thinking where people deify nature or give nature a force of its own.

    - Genesis 1:1 says that God is separate from His creation, He is not part of it. He existed first and then He created the world. He is before and after it.

3. **Polytheism** teaches that there are a multiplicity of gods. The Greeks, Romans and nearly every ancient people as well as many of the primitive peoples today (Africa, South America, etc.) are polytheists.

    - Genesis 1:1 says that only ONE God created all things.

4. **Materialism** is the basis for most modern thinking. It says that matter is eternal and that matter is the only thing that exists. Communism was based on materialism with its main idea being how to distribute it equitably.

    - Genesis 1:1 says that matter had a beginning. At some point it did not exist and then God brought it into existence.

5. **Dualism**, an ancient idea developed into different systems by Plato and later Descartes. Basically, it says that there are two powers at work in the universe (good and evil) and that the interaction of these two is responsible for all of what we see (Hinduism also explains the beginning of the world as the interaction of two entities).

    - Genesis 1:1 states that everything we see was created by only ONE power: God. The Bible accounts for evil, but evil is never at the same level as God. There is only one supreme power at work according to Genesis and it was manifested at the very beginning.

6. **Humanism** teaches that man is the ultimate reality; there is nothing higher or nobler than man. Many good works are done to benefit mankind, and they're done because of people who hold to this philosophy.

    - Genesis 1:1 refutes this idea because it teaches that God, not man, is the ultimate being since He was here before man and that God is the creator of man, and not the other way around.

7. **Evolution**, our most prevalent idea today, says that the effect of time and chance interfacing with eternal matter is responsible for the universe.

    - Genesis 1:1 says that in the beginning (specific time), God (not chance) created it (not evolution), the heavens and the earth.

7 Theories that are Destroyed by Genesis 1:1

1. **Naturalism** teaches that all is matter, but Genesis teaches that all is matter

2. **Deism** says that God created things and then was not involved. Genesis goes on to describe God's involvement with mankind.

3. **Agnosticism** (supposing that we can't know) is destroyed by Genesis 1:1, because we do know. The Bible tells us what has happened to create the situation that the world is in.

4. **Monism**, which teaches a genesis without God (everything just happened). Genesis, however, doesn't say that everything just happened. Genesis teaches that God made these things happen.

5. **Determinism** says it's all fate. Genesis 1:1 doesn't talk about fate, it talks about a deliberate, willful action. God created the world.

6. **Pragmatism** teaches that whatever works is what is best. Genesis 1:1 says God willingly created something objectively, which is the creation.

7. **Nihilism** - simple might makes right. Genesis demonstrates that God's might is what created the world.

All of these various human ideas are different ways to deny the simple truth of Genesis 1:1 and replace it with a man-made idea.

The Words in Genesis 1:1

We will save the phrase "in the beginning" for later when we will discuss the age of the earth.

God

The Hebrew term "Elohim" stresses the majesty and omnipotence of God. It is a plural noun (gods) but used in a singular fashion in this verse. This immediately suggests the dynamic nature of God who is at the same time one yet more than one, somehow.

Created

The word created refers to the unique work of God, never used with humans as the subject. The word means to call into existence from nothing. Man "forms" or "fashions," but only God "creates." The whole system of faith rests here: either random particles which always existed, generated by themselves a more complex, orderly universe and then graduated to intelligent beings capable of applying and developing intelligence (i.e. the same matter that made a rock made you); or God created it. This is the choice we have to make.

Heavens

This does not refer to the stars and planets but to the space where these are situated. When we refer to our existence, we talk about the "space – mass – time" universe, the basic components of our existence. These "heavens" would refer to the space component since the time component has been introduced (in the beginning) and the mass element is about to follow. No word is used in the Bible to express this idea of space and so the term "heavens" is used, as in the idea of expanse or universe.

Earth

Again, there is no word in the Bible that refers to "matter," so Moses uses the term earth (land) which describes the creation of the next basic component which is matter (not yet shaped or formed but now in existence).

In the Beginning

I have said that the universe is a combination of the elements of space, matter and time. Science teaches that each of these elements is necessary for the universe to have a meaningful existence:

- If there is space and time but no matter, then the universe is empty and nothing happens.

- If there is matter (which includes energy) and time but no space, there is no movement, just one big mass. Space is needed.

- Time is the third and most important component because it permits perception of the matter and space. Genesis 1:1 says that the element of time was called into existence along with space and matter to comprise the time-space-matter continuum which we call the universe.

Now, Genesis says that this time-space-matter component was not yet formed. The following verses go on to explain how God fashioned the raw materials of creation into the universe that we now see.

Some authors say that verse 1 is the title of Genesis or a summary of events, but as we said before, the summary of Genesis 1 is given in chapter 2:4.

> ...these are the generations of the heavens and the earth when they were created.

- Also, all the other sections of Genesis have no titles, only these summary statements showing the end of a particular generation.

- So, the first act of the first day of creation was the bringing forth the building blocks of the universe, the time-space-matter elements.

If you were translating Genesis 1:1 into modern scientific English, you could say,

The transcendent, omnipotent Godhead called into existence the time-space-matter universe.

With this one verse committed to memory, all of these related ideas are stored as well. In the next chapter we will examine the passage that sets the overall theme and explains what the Bible is all about.

PASSAGE #2
GENESIS 3:1-24
GOD'S PROMISE TO FALLEN MAN

The first verse of these seven (Genesis 1:1), provides the information concerning the origin of the world (God created it through His word and power).

The second of the seven, Genesis 3:1-24, provides the explanation for how the world and the human race came to be in their present condition. This is a long passage but easy to remember because it is a narrative involving four individuals: God, Satan, Adam and Eve. In its 24 verses, three key ideas are introduced that will inform all that will be written afterwards:

Key Idea #1 - The Reason for Mankind and the Creation's Fallen State

At some point in life people realize that they are not perfect and that they live in a world where others are imperfect, and that the natural world around them is also flawed and dysfunctional. People write books, songs and make movies based on the fallen nature of mankind and the slow but steady degeneration of the environment. The Bible, however, reveals that the original cause for both the imperfect world and fallen nature of humanity is disobedience to God's commands, which is sin. It also details sin's destructive consequences.

These truths are eloquently and concisely wrapped together in the origin story of Adam and Eve's temptation and fall.

> Now the serpent was more crafty than any beast of the field which the Lord God had made.
> – Genesis 3:1a

We only learn about the serpent's true identity (Satan) later on in the Bible (John 8:44, Revelation 12:9). In this scene, however, the serpent is presented as being crafty and his deceitful nature is immediately on display as he begins to speak.

> And he said to the woman, "Indeed, has God said, 'You shall not eat from any tree of the garden'?"
> – Genesis 3:1b

Verse 1b begins with not just a question, but a subtle questioning of God's authority and goodness (i.e. "Has God really said this? Is He really serious about this command?"), the inference, of course, suggesting that God had denied them something that could be good for Eve and Adam.

The method is the same today. The temptation to doubt that God really means what He says and the suggestion that what God forbids is actually good and pleasant continues to draw mankind into disobedience of God's commands with similar disastrous results.

In the garden, there were two special trees (the tree of life and the tree of knowledge of good and evil), one tree prepared Adam and Eve for the other. If they did not eat of one, they would get to eat of the other. The lesson that free will needed to learn was that obedience to God's laws resulted in eternal life. Adam and Eve failed to learn that lesson and Genesis chapter 3 contains the story of that failure. Dr. Henry Morris in his book, *The Genesis Record*, calls it, "Eve's Five Mistakes."

Mistake #1 – She Compromised with a Rebel

> The woman said to the serpent,
> - Genesis 3:2a

Not only did Eve respond to a rebel sinner and try to reason with him, she became part of the rebellion by condescending to talk with him. She should have rebuked him. She tolerated the serpent's challenge to the order of things and began immediately to take a weaker position. She should have acted like Michael the archangel who, when in dispute with the devil, simply declared, "The Lord rebuke you!" (Jude 9); he did not engage.

Mistake #2 – She Changed God's Word

> [2b]"From the fruit of the trees of the garden we may eat; [3] but from the fruit of the tree which is in the middle of the garden, God has said, 'You shall not eat from it or touch it, or you will die.'"
> – Genesis 3:2b-3

She attempted to correct the serpent's question, but in her answer we see that the damage had already been done. In her reply she both added and subtracted from God's word. She made God out to be more restricting and demanding than He really was, thus reinforcing what Satan was suggesting.

God said, "You may freely eat...", Eve said, "We may eat..." God gave them full rights and abundance but she said that they simply had access. Eve added that they were forbidden to touch, however, God did not restrict touching. To examine and understand what was forbidden was permitted. It was partaking that was forbidden.

Changing God's word to either be too strict or too liberal is wrong. We tend to think that being too strict is a safeguard against liberalism, but to change God's word in either direction is a violation. She was too strict, but this did not protect her from eventually disobeying God's command.

Mistake #3 – She Considered the Offer

> [4] The serpent said to the woman, "You surely will not die! [5] For God knows that in the day you eat from it your eyes will be opened, and you will be like God, knowing good and evil." [6] When the woman saw that the tree was good for food, and that it was a delight to the eyes, and that the tree was desirable to make one wise,
> - Genesis 3:4-6a

Had Eve rebuked Satan at this point, the matter would have been closed and history much different. Note that the temptation was the same one that led to Satan's own fall, "You will be like God" (Isaiah 14:12-15).

Eve discussed the matter with Satan, thus considering his proposal. This made him even more aggressive. When you do not put down someone's evil idea or action, they become more ambitious and are emboldened to win you over. At this point Satan did not simply question the law, he actually accused God of jealousy and dishonesty:

- **Liar** – It is not that you will die, it is that you will be like God.

- **Jealous** – He lied to you because He does not want you to be like Him.

He made the way of the curse the way of the blessing (i.e. good is evil and evil is good). God said that if they would refrain from the tree of good and evil, they would eat of the tree of life. Satan told them the opposite. In "considering" the offer, she was opening herself up for temptation at three levels:

- Physical temptation - "good for food." Something that appeals to the senses, pleasure, etc.

- Emotional temptation - "pleasant to the eyes." Something beautiful aesthetically, something that moves you.

- Spiritual temptation - "desirable to make wise." An appeal to one's mind, intellect and pride. To have special insight or vision.

John talks about these three areas of temptation:

> For all that is in the world, the lust of the flesh and the lust of the eyes and the boastful pride of life, is not from the Father, but is from the world.
> – I John 2:16

Jesus faced the same threefold temptations in the desert:

> [1] Jesus, full of the Holy Spirit, returned from the Jordan and was led around by the Spirit in the wilderness [2] for forty days, being tempted by the devil. And He ate nothing during those days, and when they had ended, He became hungry. [3] And the devil said to Him, "If You are the Son of God, tell this stone to become bread." [4] And Jesus answered him, "It is written, 'Man shall not live on bread alone.'"
> [5] And he led Him up and showed Him all the kingdoms of the world in a moment of time. [6] And the devil said to Him, "I will give You all this domain and its glory; for

> it has been handed over to me, and I give it to whomever I wish. ⁷Therefore if You worship before me, it shall all be Yours." ⁸Jesus answered him, "It is written, 'You shall worship the Lord your God and serve Him only.'"
> ⁹And he led Him to Jerusalem and had Him stand on the pinnacle of the temple, and said to Him, "If You are the Son of God, throw Yourself down from here; ¹⁰for it is written,
> 'He will command His angels concerning You to guard You,' ¹¹and,
> 'On their hands they will bear You up,
> So that You will not strike Your foot against a stone.'"
> ¹²And Jesus answered and said to him, "It is said, 'You shall not put the Lord your God to the test.'"
> - Luke 4:1-12

- Physical appetite: bread when hungry.

- Emotional desire: possession of the world and its kingdoms.

- Spiritual pride: special protection by the angels.

Eve was attacked at all three levels at once and she seriously considered these things without thought of the consequences. What should she have done?

Stand Firm with the Armor of God (Ephesians 6:11)

A rebuke, a firm stand not to compromise, a stand based on the protection of God's armor which is the Word and Spirit. Her response should not have been a discussion, consideration or a negotiation, but rather a firm stand.

> ...Resist the devil and he will flee from you.
> – James 4:7

Run Away

> Now flee from youthful lusts and pursue righteousness, faith, love and peace, with those who call on the Lord from a pure heart.
> – II Timothy 2:22

Psychologists tell us that we have two basic instincts when facing danger and that is to fight or run away. Depending on the circumstances and our assessment of the situation, we usually choose one or the other. Sometimes the temptation is too great for our strength, sometimes we may be misunderstood. It is better to run away than to risk being seduced.

> Better a live dog than a dead lion.
> - Ecclesiastes 9:4

Eve did neither of these. She did not make a strong stand nor run away for protection. She shopped, she admired, she considered, she said to herself, "Why not?"

Mistake #4 – She Disobeyed (Challenged)

> ... she took from its fruit and ate;
> - Genesis 3:6b

No matter what Satan said, no matter how attracted she was, no matter how mixed up the serpent made the situation, the bottom line was that with her own mouth she had said that she understood what God's instruction was: Do not eat the fruit!

Here is where her free will came into play. She chose to believe Satan regarding the situation rather than God. She liked the devil's explanation of how things were more than what God said about how things were.

There was nothing in Eve that pushed her to sin, no weakness of flesh (like us) that led her to sin. She sinned because she chose to disregard God's word. Although her sin was more serious (she had received "much"), it was not any different than our own disobedience today. We sin when we challenge or disregard God with our contempt for His commands.

Mistake #5 – She Led Adam to sin

> And she gave also to her husband with her, and he ate.
> – Genesis 3:6c

As a prototype of all sinners, once Eve had sinned, she led Adam to sin with her. She went from being God's defender to being Satan's helper. One question that often comes up at this point is the following:

Why did Adam also eat?

There may have been many reasons: because he loved her, because he wanted to share in her punishment. This, of course, would make Adam noble in sinning and this concept is not a biblical one. We do not know, therefore, what went through his mind other than the fact that he was not deceived like the woman (I Timothy 2:14). All we do know is that he also chose to disobey God. He probably had the same arguments put to him by his wife rather than by the serpent. Eve was deceived because Satan, in the guise of a serpent, seduced her. Adam, on the other hand, was convinced by the person he knew and loved. He may have thought that all was lost (which demonstrated both the weakness of his faith and lack of trust in

God). Either way, the result was disobedience to God and the consequences of that disobedience.

Summary #1

Note that Eve's five mistakes are a preview of the stages that each of us go through when we fall into sin because of temptation:

1. Failure to rebuke sin when it appears

Sinfulness is usually attractive, desirable or powerful, and our lack of quick and decisive action at its first appearance is usually our downfall. Effective rebuke requires three things:

- Knowledge of what is truly good and evil (knowledge provided by God's word).
- Conviction of our own position (the rightness and value of obeying God).
- Immediate response (recognizing and denouncing sin as sin immediately).

2. Compromising God's word

When we want to sin and still remain Christians, we simply change what God's word says. "Christian" homosexuals, for example, have their own theologians, commentaries and churches that support their lifestyle and shape their religion around it. If we want to continue our bad habits we simply "block out" the parts in the Bible that deal with them or find a group that will accept and even applaud our sin.

3. Considering the pleasure of sin

When we do not rebuke sin immediately, we are more inclined to examine and experience it. The salesman's basic approach is always to encourage you to try the product (of course this is acceptable when purchasing a car or some other item), however, it leads to disaster when the "product" in question is sin. Contemplating sin often leads to acting out sin.

4. Consent

If we do not initially refuse to sin, we will eventually give in to it. The most successful strategy is to decide ahead of time what you will do when confronted with temptation. This leaves no room for hesitation when tempted, only an automatic decision to reject the temptation and move past it through right action and prayer.

5. Start a club

Once we have given in to temptation, the next step is usually to find a sympathetic partner who will let us sin in peace or join us. Paul mentions this phenomena in Romans 1:32. The Apostle says that the eventual state is that sinners, who know they are doing wrong, encourage others to do wrong and even applaud them in their evil actions thus justifying their own disobedience somehow.

Summary #2

In the first section of passage #2 (Genesis 3:1-6), we find the reasons why mankind and the creation are in their fallen state.

- Adam and Eve disobeyed God's command and by exercising their free will in this manner have separated themselves from Him.

- This separation from God (eventually resulting in death) is the direct and automatic result of disobedience or sin against God.

- The natural consequences of separation from God are decay, destruction and the extinguishing of life (i.e. unplug a lamp from its power source and it will no longer be able to produce light; cut a branch away from its tree and the branch will in time decay, dry up and eventually return to dust). In the same way, separating a human being from God through sin will result in that person's eventual physical death and the eternal separation of their spirit from God.

Thankfully, not all is darkness. In Genesis 3:7-24 we read that God makes a promise to destroy the source of sin and evil in the world. Before examining this promise, however, let us first review the consequences of sin experienced by Adam and Eve.

The Consequences of Sin — Genesis 3:7-24

Genesis records, in sequence, the consequences and events that took place after the disobedience of Adam and Eve:

1. Shame

> Then the eyes of both of them were opened, and they knew that they were naked;
> - Genesis 3:7a

They knew from experience (they tasted the fruit) the knowledge of good and evil. They had experienced good and now they were experiencing evil. Their experience of evil began with the shame that comes from knowingly disobeying God.

We wonder why their nakedness was the focal point of their shame, since their sin was not sexual in nature. One explanation is that they understood that as "head" of the human race, they had corrupted future generations by their sin. Their reproductive organs, which symbolized the future of humanity, became a visual reminder of their sin and its consequences.

Another idea is that they realized that they could not hide their sin and their nakedness was a confirmation of this.

Either way, the Bible says that they felt embarrassment and shame for having done wrong.

2. Guilt

> ...and they sewed fig leaves together and made themselves loin coverings.
> - Genesis 3:7b

The fact that they tried to cover themselves means that they felt guilty. They knew that they had done wrong and felt badly about it, which is probably what saved them. Had they been proud like Satan, God could have destroyed them then and there.

Note the inadequacy of trying to cover themselves; they covered themselves but still experienced fear. Guilty people make great efforts at self-justification, which never succeeds in covering the fear or shame they feel for what they have done. However, when God covered Adam and Eve, they were no longer afraid and, though guilty, could function once again.

3. Fear

> [8]They heard the sound of the Lord God walking in the garden in the cool of the day, and the man and his wife hid themselves from the presence of the Lord God among the trees of the garden. [9]Then the Lord God called to the man, and said to him, "Where are you?" [10]He said, "I heard the sound of You in the garden, and I was afraid because I was naked; so I hid myself."
> - Genesis 3:8-10

Shame and guilt produce fear. Fear because a feature of man's conscience (where his will operates) is that man intuitively knows that sin begets punishment. God declares that disobedience brings death and knowledge of this primal spiritual law is part of man's psyche (Romans 1:28-32).

The normal fellowship between Adam and God could not abide sin. Adam knew God's will concerning sin and, consequently, was afraid of the judgment he knew would come. He was not afraid because of his physical nakedness; he was afraid because his nakedness now reminded him of sin and its consequence: death.

4. More sin

> [11] And He said, "Who told you that you were naked? Have you eaten from the tree of which I commanded you not to eat?" [12] The man said, "The woman whom You gave to be with me, she gave me from the tree, and I ate." [13] Then the LORD God said to the woman, "What is this you have done?" And the woman said, "The serpent deceived me, and I ate."
> - Genesis 3:11-13

It does not take long for sin to multiply. Adam immediately begins to show signs of his moral deterioration. When asked about the tree, instead of confessing and asking for forgiveness, Adam does two things: he blames his wife and then he blames God. Instead of praising God for His goodness, he now blames Him for his troubles!

When posed with the same question, Eve does not acknowledge guilt or ask for forgiveness, she blames the serpent and offers the excuse that she was deceived by him (instead of acknowledging that she had disobeyed God).

Sin has already reduced them to denying their own guilt and blinded them to God's goodness. This is seen in the fact that neither of them appealed to God for help.

5. Judgment

The first thing they learn about evil is that it always results in judgment and punishment by God. God pronounces judgment in the same order that the sin proceeded: Satan, Eve and then Adam.

A. Satan is judged

> [14]The LORD God said to the serpent,
> "Because you have done this,
> Cursed are you more than all cattle,
> And more than every beast of the field;
> On your belly you will go,
> And dust you will eat
> All the days of your life;
> [15]And I will put enmity
> Between you and the woman,
> And between your seed and her seed;
> He shall bruise you on the head,
> And you shall bruise him on the heel."
> - Genesis 3:14-15

The snake's posture (whatever it may have been before) will now be that of one slithering in the dust, trampled underfoot by other animals. This is the imagery of Satan's position, he who once was an angel! Now he will be hated and will produce fear and repulsion, as snakes do in normal circumstances.

We get a glimpse of Satan's overall plan when we hear the details of the curse put on him. God places special emphasis on Satan's inability from here forward to dominate woman and specifically the offspring she will bear (which was probably the reason why he attacked her and not Adam in the first place).

God says that there will be war, not subjugation, between the woman, her children and Satan. It is interesting to note that in the Bible, men have seed not women, and spirit-beings have no seed. Spirits do not procreate, only humans do this. The seed of woman, therefore, is Jesus who was conceived without a human male but by the power of the Holy Spirit (Matthew 1:18). The seed of Satan is the "man of lawlessness, the antichrist" to whom Satan gives power and who will be destroyed by Christ's coming (II Thessalonians 2:8).

The "bruising" is a blow. For the woman's seed, the blow will be on the heel (the inferior part of the body), this is Satan's attack that resulted in the human death of Christ that was only temporary. For Satan's seed, however, the blow will be to the head, the superior part of the body and thus, fatal.

Jesus, when He returns, destroys death and will pronounce judgment on Satan who will be thrown into the "pit" forever (Revelation 20:10). This is the promise.

B. Eve is judged

> To the woman He said,
> "I will greatly multiply
> Your pain in childbirth,
> In pain you will bring forth children;
> Yet your desire will be for your husband,
> And he will rule over you."
> - Genesis 3:16

Both Adam and Eve were painlessly brought into a perfect and sinless world. Because of this sin, the creating of future society would be marked by pain. Because of their sin, death entered the world, and pain at childbirth will become the constant reminder of this fact.

Before sin, man and woman enjoyed co-rulership over creation. Because of sin, this perfect balance was upset and God established a rule of law in the area of family leadership. The husband would rule and be the head of the family unit. This concept is repeated and confirmed in the New Testament (I Corinthians 11:3; Ephesians 5:22-24). There have been many abuses of this situation, but the Bible clarifies the loving relationship that is to exist within this union (Ephesians 5:25, 28-30).

There is also mercy in God's judgment over Eve. She will not desire the serpent and his promises, but her loyalty will now be to her husband. Also, the pain of childbirth will not overcome her love of husband and family, and there will be a limit to her suffering.

C. Adam is judged

> [17]Then to Adam He said, "Because you have listened to the voice of your wife, and have eaten from the tree about which I commanded you, saying, 'You shall not eat from it';
> Cursed is the ground because of you;
> In toil you will eat of it
> All the days of your life.
> [18]"Both thorns and thistles it shall grow for you;
> And you will eat the plants of the field;
> [19]By the sweat of your face
> You will eat bread,
> Till you return to the ground,
> Because from it you were taken;
> For you are dust,
> And to dust you shall return."
> - Genesis 3:17-19

First, God outlines the sin. Adam listened to his wife (he changed his allegiance) and not to the word of God. Loyalty to the Word is to be stronger than any human tie, including marriage. Eve did not deceive him, she convinced him (i.e. what harm could it do; only this once; I did it and nothing happened, etc.). In the end, the plain truth is that Adam did what God said not to do.

God then pronounces the judgment on Adam. Since he is the head of the race, the judgment, by extension, will affect all of his descendants. Because of what Adam has done, God must now remove Himself from the physical sphere and this will affect mankind. God is holy and sinless, and cannot dwell where there is sin and immorality. Until Adam and Eve sinned, God maintained the balance for life in the physical world by His presence.

Adam and Eve lived in a perfect world where God maintained this perfection through His power. There was no deterioration, no overpopulation and no imbalances. However, once sin entered the world, God removed His presence and thus permitted the cycle of deterioration to take place.

This was the reality of good and evil warned against. The deterioration, not permitted before, was now released. Mutations that caused decay began to form. Even in man, the cycle of deterioration would now cause his physical death. Of course, this was still before the great Flood, so the rate of decay and imbalance was slow. This explains why people lived such long lives during that time. However, once the Flood destroyed the world, man's lifespan shortened and the rate of decay accelerated because the creation was further weakened and compromised by this worldwide catastrophe. Genesis explains the symptoms and features of a declining world where God was no longer extending His power to maintain a "steady state" of life and order thus allowing all things to gradually disintegrate toward disorder and death.

God did not create death. He merely removed His life sustaining power and allowed His creation to disintegrate, which is what it would naturally do without the original life force that gave it existence to begin with. This concept of deterioration was universally observed and scientifically formulated about 100 years ago (Carnot, Clausius, Kelvin and others). It was called the Second Law of Thermodynamics. This law states that all systems, if left to themselves, become degraded or disordered. All systems, whether they be watches or suns, eventually wear out. Even modern scientists are reconfirming the universality of this law with new equipment that can observe its function in the furthest reaches of the universe and not only here on earth (e.g. Hubble telescope).

Instead of all things being "made" (organized into complex systems, as they were during creation week), they are now being "unmade" (becoming disorganized and simple). This is what is wrong with our world and the reason for its deterioration.

Let us get back to the passage in Genesis and its language. "Cursed is the ground" is the reverse of "it is very good." The difference here is that God no longer maintains it. The curse is that God now removes His sustaining power. "For thy sake" refers to God's mercy. God removes His sustaining power not only as a response to sin but also to put a limit on the wickedness resulting from sin. Better suffering and death accompanying sin than unchecked rebellion and a never-ending multiplication of wicked people using the creation for sinful purposes. Once sin was in, God had to intervene.

The curse on the earth is followed by the result that it would have on man:

1. Sorrow, continual disappointment and futility in life, especially in providing for oneself.

2. Pain and suffering (symbolized by the terms: thorns and thistles).

3. Hard work. Before, man ate of the abundance of the garden. Now, he would have to scratch a living from an uncooperative earth.

4. Death. With all of his work and effort, man would, like the rest of the creation, deteriorate into the primary elements from which he was taken, the earth itself.

This was the result of the curse on Adam. It is interesting to note that Jesus experienced every one of these elements when, as the Bible says, "He bore the curse on our behalf" (Galatians 3:13).

1. **Sorrow** - He was the man of sorrows (Isaiah 53:3).

2. **Pain** - He wore the curse as a crown of thorns (Mark 15:17).

3. **Work** - His work and labor made Him sweat, but His sweat came out as drops of blood (Luke 22:44).

4. **Death** - Finally, God brought Him into the "dust of death" (Psalms 22:15).

God placed a curse on the earth by withdrawing Himself and thus allowing the world and man to disintegrate into death. However, He did not leave the world without hope. That hope was that one day He would create a new heaven and a new earth which would never be destroyed by sin and where He would dwell eternally with His people.

Paradise Lost

Now that the judgment was pronounced, there was a response from Adam and Eve.

> Now the man called his wife's name Eve, because she was the mother of all the living.
> - Genesis 3:20

Adam renames his wife. Originally, he had named her "woman." This term signified that she was part of him, equal and similar in nature. Now he gives her another name that will mean several other things:

1. The word Eve means "life-giver." It signified that they were going to obey God's command to multiply upon the earth.

2. This response also showed that they believed God's promise to bring salvation through the seed of the woman. By bearing children despite pain, woman was expressing her belief that the savior would ultimately come.

3. God renews His relationship with man, not based on perfection anymore, but based on faith. Because they believe God's promise and express that faith in their intention to procreate, Adam and Eve are saved.

In response to their faith, expressed in obedience, God provides a covering for their shame, guilt and nakedness.

> The LORD God made garments of skin for Adam and his wife and clothed them.
> - Genesis 3:21

Note that animals were sacrificed in order to provide this covering. This is the first preview indicating how redemption would ultimately come: the blood of the innocent to cover the sins of the guilty.

> Then the LORD God said, "Behold, the man has

> become like one of Us, knowing good and evil; and now, he might stretch out his hand, and take also from the tree of life, and eat, and live forever"
> - Genesis 3:22

Man now knows, experientially, both good (fellowship with God in a perfect creation) as well as evil (separation from God and the punishment associated with evil). This is the reverse of those who will come after Adam who will experience evil first (sin and the expectation of death), and then when saved, experience good (fellowship with God and perfection through faith - salvation).

Adam is now weakened by sin and, although repentant and saved, can still be tempted to eat of the tree of life, the result being that he would continue to exist in the sin-state forever. Perhaps this is what Satan did and why there is no salvation for him.

> [23]therefore the LORD God sent him out from the garden of Eden, to cultivate the ground from which he was taken. [24]So He drove the man out; and at the east of the garden of Eden He stationed the cherubim and the flaming sword which turned every direction to guard the way to the tree of life.
> - Genesis 3:23-24

The wording suggests that Adam was reluctant to leave and so God does two things to guarantee the carrying out of His judgment. First, He drives the man and his wife out of the garden and into their new home, work and status. Second, He stations angels and a flaming sword to protect access to the tree of life. The tree is preserved for a future time. The sword signifies that you cannot access the tree of life without first experiencing physical death.

The remaining story of the Bible will describe how God worked in order to bring man to the point where he could again reach out and eat of the tree of life.

> He who has an ear, let him hear what the Spirit says to the churches. To him who overcomes, I will grant to eat of the tree of life which is in the Paradise of God.'
> - Revelation 2:7

PASSAGE #3
GENESIS 11:27-12:7
THE PERSON OF PROMISE - HISTORICAL

Up until the time of Abraham there was no information revealed directly concerning the promise made to Adam and Eve. People knew that God had spoken of a Savior of some kind but there was silence as to the time of His coming, who He would be and what He would actually do to save them.

The first revelation about these matters comes to a man called Abram who lived in the land of Ur which is modern day Iraq. The passage concerning Abram introduces the family through whom God will ultimately produce the individual who will fulfill the promise made in Genesis 3. This passage grounds in history and family what God had only promised in spirit.

Genesis 11:27 - 12:7 sets the opening scene of a storyline that will follow the human thread of the Savior's lineage from the man (Abram) first called to produce the nation from which this Savior would eventually come. The story begins by introducing a family that is in transition.

> ²⁷Now these are the records of the generations of Terah. Terah became the father of Abram, Nahor and

> Haran; and Haran became the father of Lot. ²⁸Haran died in the presence of his father Terah in the land of his birth, in Ur of the Chaldeans. ²⁹Abram and Nahor took wives for themselves. The name of Abram's wife was Sarai; and the name of Nahor's wife was Milcah, the daughter of Haran, the father of Milcah and Iscah. ³⁰Sarai was barren; she had no child.
> ³¹Terah took Abram his son, and Lot the son of Haran, his grandson, and Sarai his daughter-in-law, his son Abram's wife; and they went out together from Ur of the Chaldeans in order to enter the land of Canaan; and they went as far as Haran, and settled there. ³²The days of Terah were two hundred and five years; and Terah died in Haran.
> - Genesis 11:27-32

Note the situation:

- Haran died young.

- Nahor married his dead brother's daughter (his niece).

- Abram married his half-sister, Sarai, who is said to be barren.

We have few details, but it seems that Terah along with his son Abram, Abram's wife Sarai, and his grandson, Lot, left Ur in order to make his way to Canaan. Terah and his family only travelled as far as the city of Haran (probably built in memory of his dead son) and remained there. The story of Terah ends at this point. He may have refused to go on, he may have been sick, we do not know. All we do know is that his original destination was Canaan, but for one reason or another he never made it. This sets the scene for God's call to Abram.

> ¹Now the LORD said to Abram,
> "Go forth from your country,
> And from your relatives

> And from your father's house,
> To the land which I will show you;
> ²And I will make you a great nation,
> And I will bless you,
> And make your name great;
> And so you shall be a blessing;
> ³And I will bless those who bless you,
> And the one who curses you I will curse.
> And in you all the families of the earth will be blessed."
>
> ⁴ So Abram went forth as the LORD had spoken to him; and Lot went with him. Now Abram was seventy-five years old when he departed from Haran. ⁵Abram took Sarai his wife and Lot his nephew, and all their possessions which they had accumulated, and the persons which they had acquired in Haran, and they set out for the land of Canaan; thus they came to the land of Canaan. ⁶Abram passed through the land as far as the site of Shechem, to the oak of Moreh. Now the Canaanite was then in the land. ⁷The LORD appeared to Abram and said, "To your descendants I will give this land." So he built an altar there to the LORD who had appeared to him.
> - Genesis 12:1-7

The Lord instructs Abram to leave Haran and the things keeping him there: his country (people of that era rarely left their villages, let alone their country); his culture, language, traditions, religion; his family and friends; his work, home and land.

Abram is asked to leave everything behind, however, God makes a series of promises to him if he responds to His calling with obedience:

1. Abram will give rise to a great nation.
2. He himself will become a great man.
3. He will bless others with his life.

4. God will protect him.
5. The entire world throughout history will be blessed through Abram.

These sound like great blessings, but consider Abram's state:

A - He had to completely forsake home, family, nation and culture in order to have a great nation built from himself. In other words, he had to abandon the very things necessary to create a nation in order to have a nation come from his generation.

B - He had to abandon the safety of what was familiar in order to go into the unknown with only the promise of God's protection but no visible sign of it.

The journey to Canaan was approximately 400 miles for his family and servants along with livestock and possessions. In verse 7, the Lord "appears" to Abram. This is the first time this phenomenon (God present in the immediate physical context) is expressed in this way. We learn that God does so in order to add one more thing to the list of promises made to Abram.

6. That the land he was living in would one day be the possession of his people.

With time, God changed Abram's name (which meant "high" or "exalted father") to Abraham (which means "father of a multitude").

This passage, as one of our seven passages, identifies the source and stream of the nation that served as a cultural, religious, political and historical stage upon which the "promise," the "seed of the woman" would make His historical, physical appearance. It answers the question, "Where would this promised one come from, or what nation would produce the seed that was to defeat the evil one?" Were people to look for Him among the leading nations of history, the Egyptians perhaps, or the Greeks?

Genesis 11:27-12:7 answers that question by showing us that God selected and called only one man who was a Chaldean from the Mesopotamian region of Ur (with its own multiple deities, temples and priests), from whom He would eventually send the Savior.

God revealed Himself to this one man and set about to make of him:

1. A believer in the one, true and living God.

2. An example of the kind of faith God wanted all believers to have.

3. The human starting point for a people whose culture, religion, laws and historical experience would be a living witness of not only the promise that would be delivered through their nation (a Savior), but also the reason why the promise was made (man's guilt and condemnation due to sin), and the way that this condemnation would be removed (vicarious atonement - a concept brought to life and demonstrated through the Jewish sacrificial system which previewed how the Savior would ultimately fulfill His mission to save man from his sins).

After this passage, the entire Old Testament simply lays out the fulfillment of God's promises to Abram by describing the growth and development of Abraham's family from a single unit to 12 tribes and finally to a great nation in possession of their own land. Starting from Abraham, the Bible traces each generation throughout the centuries (along with its wars, kings, interactions with God and ongoing prophecies concerning the fulfillment of the original promise).

This third passage ties together the physical history that starts with the promise made in the garden, is then linked to the main vehicle sustaining that promise throughout history (the Jewish people beginning with Abraham) which is then connected to the appearance of Jesus, son of Joseph of Nazareth, who was himself of the tribe of Judah, a direct descendant of Abraham.

Note that I did not include the other important identity marker for Jesus which is "Son of God" because His genealogical connection to David and Judah, and then back to Abraham does not identify Him as the One fulfilling the promise – for this we must look to the prophets.

PASSAGE #4
ISAIAH 53:1-12
THE PERSON OF PROMISE - SPIRITUAL

According to different scholars, there are between 200 and 400 prophecies concerning Christ contained in the Old Testament and fulfilled by Jesus in the New Testament (Association for Bible Research). The fulfillment of prophecy is one of the major arguments for the inspiration of the Bible (i.e. only an inspired book contains fulfilled prophecy). The Bible is the only Holy Book that contains both prophecy and its confirmed fulfillment in the same text.

Beginning with Abraham, the Old Testament primarily tells the story of the Jewish nation, but interlaced with this story is the golden thread of prophecy from generation to generation that spoke of God's promise and seed to come at a certain point of both human and Jewish history. The Jews were God's chosen people, but they were chosen for a reason and that reason was to bring Christ into the world. The prophets, however, were the ones who put a face and a purpose to the person of the promise.

The fourth of the seven passages, therefore, is from one of those prophets, Isaiah.

More than any other prophet, Isaiah's prophecies concerning the Messiah described not only the character of the Savior to come but laid out the details of His actual mission in saving man from eternal condemnation.

The Messiah's Character

> [1] Who has believed our message?
> And to whom has the arm of the LORD been revealed?
> [2] For He grew up before Him like a tender shoot,
> And like a root out of parched ground;
> He has no stately form or majesty
> That we should look upon Him,
> Nor appearance that we should be attracted to Him.
> [3] He was despised and forsaken of men,
> A man of sorrows and acquainted with grief;
> And like one from whom men hide their face
> He was despised, and we did not esteem Him.
> - Isaiah 53:1-3

Isaiah begins by anticipating doubt and disbelief of the things he is about to say concerning the Messiah (i.e. that He would suffer). He goes on to describe a man who would have no natural appeal to others, and who would be considered of low esteem and rejected by most people.

> [4] Surely our griefs He Himself bore,
> And our sorrows He carried;
> Yet we ourselves esteemed Him stricken,
> Smitten of God, and afflicted.
> [5] But He was pierced through for our transgressions,
> He was crushed for our iniquities;
> The chastening for our well-being fell upon Him,
> And by His scourging we are healed.
> [6] All of us like sheep have gone astray,
> Each of us has turned to his own way;

But the LORD has caused the iniquity of us all
To fall on Him.

[7] He was oppressed and He was afflicted,
Yet He did not open His mouth;
Like a lamb that is led to slaughter,
And like a sheep that is silent before its shearers,
So He did not open His mouth.
[8] By oppression and judgment He was taken away;
And as for His generation, who considered
That He was cut off out of the land of the living
For the transgression of my people, to whom the stroke was due?
[9] His grave was assigned with wicked men,
Yet He was with a rich man in His death,
Because He had done no violence,
Nor was there any deceit in His mouth.

[10] But the LORD was pleased
To crush Him, putting Him to grief;
If He would render Himself as a guilt offering,
He will see His offspring,
He will prolong His days,
And the good pleasure of the LORD will prosper in His hand.
[11] As a result of the anguish of His soul,
He will see it and be satisfied;
By His knowledge the Righteous One,
My Servant, will justify the many,
As He will bear their iniquities.
[12] Therefore, I will allot Him a portion with the great,
And He will divide the booty with the strong;
Because He poured out Himself to death,
And was numbered with the transgressors;
Yet He Himself bore the sin of many,
And interceded for the transgressors.
- Isaiah 53:4-12

Isaiah describes the various aspects of the Messiah's suffering.

1. The manner in which He suffered. He did so quietly.

> ⁷He was oppressed and He was afflicted,
> Yet He did not open His mouth;
> Like a lamb that is led to slaughter,
> And like a sheep that is silent before its shearers,
> So He did not open His mouth.

2. The reason for His suffering. He paid the moral debt for our sins.

> ⁵But He was pierced through for our transgressions,
> He was crushed for our iniquities;
> The chastening for our well-being fell upon Him,
> And by His scourging we are healed.

3. The result of His suffering. His intercession removes the sins of those who believe in Him (which was the promise made in the garden at the beginning).

> ¹¹As a result of the anguish of His soul,
> He will see it and be satisfied;
> By His knowledge the Righteous One,
> My Servant, will justify the many,
> As He will bear their iniquities.
> ¹²Therefore, I will allot Him a portion with the great,
> And He will divide the booty with the strong;
> Because He poured out Himself to death,
> And was numbered with the transgressors;
> Yet He Himself bore the sin of many,
> And interceded for the transgressors.

4. The proof that His suffering removed sin and guilt: the resurrection.

> ¹⁰But the LORD was pleased
> To crush Him, putting Him to grief;
> If He would render Himself as a guilt offering,
> He will see His offspring,
> He will prolong His days,
> And the good pleasure of the LORD will prosper
> in His hand.

Nowhere else in Scripture do we find a more comprehensive description of the person and mission of the Messiah, exactly fulfilled some seven centuries later by Jesus Christ.

This key passage also serves as the link that connects the Old and New Testaments in our "Bible in Seven Passages" series:

A. It summarizes the information concerning the Messiah and His mission that is symbolized and described in the story of the Jewish nation including their religious system and teachings, and brings these together into a single person.

B. It points directly to a specific person (the Messiah), a specific mission (vicarious atonement), a specific result (forgiveness of sin leading to justification of the sinner and a specific vindication: resurrection). All of these are wrapped into a single person and a single event to appear and take place in the future of the Jewish nation.

C. This prophecy is so specific that it could only be fulfilled by a Jewish man living as part of the Jewish people at the time when Jesus was on earth.

Jesus Himself uses a passage from Isaiah to openly declare that He was the Messiah produced by the Jewish nation and spoken of by the Jewish prophets in the Hebrew Scriptures thus fulfilling all that was written in what we call the Old Testament and establishing, as well as confirming, the authority of the writings we refer to as the New Testament.

> [14]And Jesus returned to Galilee in the power of the Spirit, and news about Him spread through all the surrounding district. [15]And He began teaching in their synagogues and was praised by all.
> [16]And He came to Nazareth, where He had been brought up; and as was His custom, He entered the synagogue on the Sabbath, and stood up to read. [17]And the book of the prophet Isaiah was handed to Him. And He opened the book and found the place where it was written,
> [18]"The Spirit of the Lord is upon Me,
> Because He anointed Me to preach the gospel to the poor.
> He has sent Me to proclaim release to the captives,
> And recovery of sight to the blind,
> To set free those who are oppressed,
> [19]To proclaim the favorable year of the Lord."
> [20]And He closed the book, gave it back to the attendant and sat down; and the eyes of all in the synagogue were fixed on Him. [21]And He began to say to them, "Today this Scripture has been fulfilled in your hearing."
> - Luke 4:14-21

Summary

In the effort to summarize and maintain the key information and message of the Bible in only seven passages, the ones we have looked at in this study have provided the following information:

Genesis 11:27-12:7 (Passage #3)

This passage describes the way God fulfilled His promise to save sinful man (through the agency of a person born of a nation specifically chosen and formed by God for this very reason). The Savior will be a descendant of Abraham and the Old Testament will describe how this nation will eventually produce this person.

Isaiah 53:1-12 (Passage #4)

The passage in Isaiah describes the Messiah, His mission, the results of His mission and the way to verify His credibility. Isaiah's prophecy brings together the ultimate purpose of the creation of the Jewish nation (to produce the Messiah) with the ultimate purpose of the Messiah (to save mankind from spiritual death), and these two projected to a definite future time, place and person.

With the study of these two passages complete, we can now move on to the final three sections which are all found in the New Testament.

PASSAGE #5
JOHN 3:14-16
THE PROMISE REVEALED

In a future time where all the dreams of technology have been realized:

- Driverless transportation.

- Personalized on-demand delivery of everything from food and clothing to furniture and personal services including entertainment, education, even medical attention brought to your door by contacting the Universal Services link for your sector and placing your request for products or services.

- Everything you need and everything you want in every imaginable version, available for delivery. For example:

    o Feel like Italian food? – Universal Services will send a team to set the table and prep a delicious Italian menu and mood in your own home.

    o Need a blood test or MRI? – Universal Services will send their mobile lab and X-ray unit to take care of your medical needs anywhere or time that is convenient for you.

- o Vacation in Greece? – Universal Services will book your flight, process your security requirements, send the shuttle to pick you up and deliver you to the plane's entry door. No waiting in line, no checkpoints, no stress about being late – you can even have U.S.'s bag packing service prep your suitcases for automatic check-in at the airport before you leave.

As I mentioned in the first chapter of this book, this society of the future has succeeded in integrating the government, major media and technology companies with universities and the military to create a unified system to gather, manage, store and disseminate information of all kinds.

This gathering and centralizing of information has led to breakthroughs in developing, perfecting and producing all kinds of advances in food production, transportation, engineering and the manufacturing of new and exciting products and services. However, there has been one ominous development, especially for Christians.

The centralization of information and the control of what ideas and books are stored and transferred from the Quantum Memory Storage Units which are responsible for archiving and distributing all digital information created and exchanged in society; this centralized information bank no longer contains or distributes any material concerning the Bible.

This means that since the Bible was judged to be harmful to society because it contained hate literature (e.g. forbidding certain types of sexual activity) and promoted divisiveness (e.g. it taught that non-believers would not go to heaven); the Inclusion Committee categorized the Bible as subversive propaganda and removed it from the list of approved communication. The end result of this action has been the systematic removal of the Bible from all libraries, bookstores, schools and homes. All material, whether hard copies or digital versions of not only the Bible, but books and other types of printed material about the Bible have slowly but surely been gathered and destroyed.

In this future time and place, the Bible and all related works are being purged to the point where even Christians have little to no access to a complete Bible, let alone commentaries or other study aids that are used along with the Scriptures. This scenario produced the question, "How would believers maintain their faith in a world where the Bible was being eliminated from public access?"

One method, I suggested, would be to select certain key passages that would summarize the Bible's core message originally laid out in its 66 individual books. This is the idea behind, "The Bible in Seven Passages."

So far, we have examined the first four of these seven passages which were taken from the Old Testament:

Genesis 1:1 – Prelude to the promise: creation. This passage reveals how the world was created and by whom.

Genesis 3:1-24 – God's promise to fallen man. This passage explains the reason for the fallen nature of man and the creation as well as God's solution to man's condition: the promise of a Savior.

Genesis 11:27-12:7 – The person of promise – historical. This passage introduced Abram (Abraham) the person God chose to form a nation through whom the Savior, who would fulfill God's promise to sinful man, would come.

Isaiah 53:1-12 – The person of promise – spiritual. This passage describes the spiritual nature and mission of the person sent by God to fulfill His promise to the Jews and through them to all the world.

We will now study passage #5 in the series, this time from the New Testament, John 3:14-16, where Jesus clearly reveals the details of the promise.

The Promise Revealed — John 3:14-16

In order to understand the New Testament in its proper context, one has to know the purpose of its parts. For example:

- **The Gospels** – These are four eyewitness records of Old Testament prophecies (concerning God's promise) being fulfilled by and through Jesus and His ministry.

- **The Book of Acts** – An account of the establishment of the church from various eye witness sources recorded by Luke, a Gentile convert to Christianity.

- **The Epistles** – Letters written by various inspired Apostles and disciples containing teaching, instruction, admonitions and encouragement sent to different churches and individuals.

- **Revelation** – A record of the Apostle John's visions concerning the church and its battle with satanic forces on earth and in the spiritual realm which it wins in the end.

> ^{14}As Moses lifted up the serpent in the wilderness, even so must the Son of Man be lifted up; ^{15}so that whoever believes will in Him have eternal life. ^{16}"For God so loved the world, that He gave His only begotten Son, that whoever believes in Him shall not perish, but have eternal life.
> - John 3:14-16

In passage #5, John 3:14-16, we have Jesus, the promised One brought forth by the Jewish nation, summarizing in a single passage the content and completion of God's original promise to Adam and Eve, His covenant with Abraham and his descendants, and the fulfillment of prophecy concerning the mission of the promised One.

All of these things are contained in what some refer to as the "golden verse" of the Bible, John 3:14-16. Jesus explains in John 3:5 that salvation requires water and the Spirit, and in John 3:14-16 He refers to salvation in two other ways:

A. Born again

B. Entry to the kingdom of God

Jesus explains these things to a Jewish teacher called Nicodemus who had come to see and question Him in secret because of his fear of the Jewish leadership. Nicodemus does not understand, thinking that the term "born again" refers to human birth:

> Nicodemus said to Him, "How can a man be born when he is old? He cannot enter a second time into his mother's womb and be born, can he?"
> - John 3:4

Jesus then frames the idea of salvation in a way that Nicodemus, a Jewish Pharisee, could understand.

> [14]As Moses lifted up the serpent in the wilderness, even so must the Son of Man be lifted up; [15]so that whoever believes will in Him have eternal life.
> - John 3:14-15

Jesus refers to an incident that occurred while the Jews wandered in the desert.

> ⁶The LORD sent fiery serpents among the people and they bit the people, so that many people of Israel died. ⁷So the people came to Moses and said, "We have sinned, because we have spoken against the LORD and you; intercede with the LORD, that He may remove the serpents from us." And Moses interceded for the people. ⁸Then the LORD said to Moses, "Make a fiery serpent, and set it on a standard; and it shall come about, that everyone who is bitten, when he looks at it, he will live." ⁹And Moses made a bronze serpent and set it on the standard; and it came about,
>
> that if a serpent bit any man, when he looked to the bronze serpent, he lived.
> - Numbers 21:6-9

With this incident familiar to Jews, Jesus is teaching Nicodemus the basics of the gospel using an event from Jewish history. The people bitten by fiery snakes die, just like those guilty of sin also die (Nicodemus would understand this). The cure for the snake bite, however, was not the offering of an animal sacrifice but the obedience of faith. If they believed what Moses said (...those who looked at the bronze serpent attached to a standard or pole, would be healed) and obeyed based on that faith, they would be healed.

Jesus establishes the idea from a passage in the Hebrew Scriptures that Nicodemus could relate to, that salvation is obtained or received on the basis of faith. The faith produced the obedience which led to the salvation.

Jesus then goes one step further to explain and declare how this system of faith is related to Himself.

> For God so loved the world, that He gave His only begotten Son, that whoever believes in Him shall not perish, but have eternal life."
> - John 3:16

This passage connects back to the four Old Testament Scriptures we have studied by giving a name, a mission and the motivation for the promise made to Adam and Eve, passed forward by Abraham, carried throughout history by the Jews, spoken of by the prophets and now being fulfilled by Jesus Christ.

Let's break the passage down and unpack all the information it provides in one short verse, John 3:16.

A. God

- This tells us Who.
- The promise, in the end, comes from God.
- We read in Genesis 1:1, God created the heavens and the earth.
- We read in Genesis 3:1-24, God promises to send someone to defeat Satan.
- We read in Genesis 11:27-12:7, God spoke and made a promise to Abraham.
- We read in Isaiah 53:1-7, God spoke through the prophets concerning the Savior.
- And now, through Jesus, we see that God the Father is again the One who will complete the plan to save mankind.

B. So loved the world

- This section goes to motivation. Why did God do this?

- Agape love was and is His motivation.
- Even though mankind has fallen away into sin, God remains the same – God is love! (I John 4:8).
- Love is His great motivation.

Everyone has sin and will be condemned for it. God's love for us is what motivates His plan to save sinners from their sins. The word "so" in regards to love explains that the love required to achieve this end was such that only God could possess and express it and was beyond man's capabilities to do so.

C. That He gave His only begotten Son

- This explains the extent of God's love.
- The depth of His love is measured by the value of what He gave in order to secure our salvation.
    - He gave His one of a kind (what only-begotten means) Son.
    - Jesus, the second person in the Godhead, became a man to carry out the Father's plan.
- The Father gave Jesus up to the indignities of human suffering and death as well as the pain of separation from Himself in order to remove the guilt and condemnation man was due to suffer.
- No living being could pay such a price in the expression of love.

D. That whoever believes in Him shall not perish

- The secret of the promise is revealed here.
- Since Adam and Eve, we knew that it was sin that led to destruction and death.

- Here, Jesus reveals that it is faith in the promised One sent by God that will save mankind from death and destruction.

- Abraham and the Jewish nation as well as the prophets knew that the promised One was coming and bringing salvation.

- Jesus, however, finally revealed the who (Himself) and the how (faith) of that salvation.

E. ... but have eternal life.

- Jesus not only reveals the who and the how but the what of salvation: resurrection and eternal life experienced by every believer.

- Peter says that no one knew the details of God's promise, not even the angels (I Peter 1:13).

- Jesus clearly reveals the sum of all the prophecies and symbolism of Jewish temple worship in one succinct passage that reveals the entire plan of God to save sinful man.

> For God so loved the world, that He gave His only begotten Son, that whoever believes in Him shall not perish, but have eternal life.
> - John 3:16

PASSAGE #6
ROMANS 6:1-14
THE PROMISE REALIZED

Let us quickly review five of the seven passages that attempt to summarize the content of the Bible. Seven passages that contain enough information, so that in an emergency situation like the one described in this book, a Christian could convert a non-believer and keep faith alive until death. The five summary passages chosen so far are:

1. Genesis 1:1 – Creation
2. Genesis 3:1-24 – God's promise to fallen man
3. Genesis 11:27-12:7 – The person of the promise – historical
4. Isaiah 53:1-12 – The person of the promise – spiritual
5. John 3:14-16 – The promise revealed

Romans 6:1-14 — The Promise Realized

This passage is not actually part of the gospel message but rather a defense of the way God's promise to man was realized and worked out in a believer's life. Before examining it more closely, it is helpful to review the reasons why Paul had to actually provide this information.

Satan Attacks the Promise

We need to remember that it all began with a lie. The promise from God to send a Savior was made because Eve believed Satan's first lie.

"You surely will not die!" Genesis 3:4 – Satan seduced the woman with the promise of knowledge and an elevated position equal to God based on the false notion (on a lie) that not only had God lied to her about the fruit of the tree of the knowledge of good and evil, He did so out of selfishness (i.e. He did not want Adam and Eve to attain their full potential).

It is interesting to note that what the serpent (Satan) suggested, that Eve was missing out on knowledge and an elevated position, was similar to the things that he himself had, because of sinful pride, aspired to and for which he had been cast down by God:

> "I will ascend above the heights of the clouds;
> I will make myself like the Most High."
> - Isaiah 14:14

> "Your heart became proud on account of your beauty, and you corrupted your wisdom because of your splendor."
> - Ezekiel 28:17

His lie led to the fall of Adam and Eve, but in His judgment on them, God included a promise that the seed of woman (a person born of a woman without the participation of a man) would destroy the evil one thus freeing mankind from sin – Genesis 3:15).

Satan had seriously damaged man and the creation, but with His promise, God had limited that damage and set into motion the plan to ultimately redeem mankind. Because of this Satan now focused his efforts on the delay or the destruction of God's promise because its completion meant his own annihilation.

The history of the Jewish nation in the Old Testament: their wars, setbacks, times of glory as well as periods of wickedness and descent into idolatry, all of these tell the story of Satan's attempts to delay or destroy the people who were carrying forth God's promise of eventual salvation.

Once Jesus arrived (the promise born as a man), Satan continued in his lies to discredit or destroy Jesus Himself. From the temptations in the desert to His death on the cross, Jesus was subjected to unrelenting attacks by Satan and those he influenced. The resurrection of Jesus was the clear sign that Satan had failed, but this did not deter him from continuing his assault on Christ and those who believed in Him.

Not long after the gospel was preached and the church established, the pattern of obstruction and attempt to undermine began once again. We see Satan's aggression in many instances:

- The Apostles arrested, beaten and threatened not to preach the gospel – Acts 4-5

- The killing of Stephen – Acts 7

- General persecution of the church by the Jews – Acts 9

- Persecution and arrest of Paul – Acts 21-27

- General persecution of the church by the Romans – II Timothy 4:6

And yet, despite all of this, the church flourished and grew throughout the Roman Empire and beyond, to the point that today 2.4 billion people, 33% of the world's population, are believers.

The attacks on the church continue to this day as well. It is estimated that nearly 245 million Christians experience high levels of persecution for their faith (opendoorsusa.org). This oppression occurs in mostly Muslim countries.

However, Satan's most dangerous attack is not against people or the buildings where they meet, but against what Christians teach and live by, God's word. This was the target of the first lie in the garden as the devil first cast doubt on what God had spoken.

> "Indeed, has God said, 'You shall not eat from any tree in the garden?'"
> - Genesis 3:1b

This strategy continued throughout the history of the Jewish nation with false prophets and idolaters crediting their words and teachings as coming from God, when in reality they were doing Satan's work.

- From King Ahab's false prophets – I Kings 22:10-28
- To the prophets of Baal – Jeremiah 2:8
- Also evident in the New Testament: Bar-Jesus (Elymas) – Acts 13:6-12

The false prophets and teachers even infiltrated the church in an attempt to destroy it from within.

As far as Satan is concerned, destroying or compromising God's word in some way will succeed in stopping everything else because the promise is embodied, empowered and fully realized in and through God's word. In other words, destroy the Word and you destroy Christianity and everything it supports.

In the first century, the Bible mentions two groups that seriously threatened the unity and the spiritual peace possessed by churches of that era:

1. Judaizers, whose false teachings were directed primarily at Gentile converts to Christianity.

2. Gnostic teachers, whose false doctrines influenced all believers.

The Judaizers basically taught that you had to become a Jew before you could become a Christian, and if you were a Christian you were required to keep various parts of the Law of Moses. This required circumcision and the obeying of food laws and other ordinances not given by Jesus or the Apostles.

The Gnostic teachers taught that they had a superior gospel and if disciples followed them, they would be privy to their "hidden" or secret gospel and its practices that included restrictions on food and marriage. The idea here was that those following these leaders would no longer receive the teachings of Paul, a genuine Apostle chosen by Jesus!

When reading Paul's instruction in Romans 6:1-14, we recognize that he is responding to the two lies that were circling around the gospel at this critical time in the church's development, falsehoods that endangered the stability of young churches. One threatened to change how to respond to the gospel and the other actually tried to change the gospel itself!

Our sixth passage, Romans 6:1-14, destroys these two attempts to change or compromise and thus destroy the gospel's content or as Paul refers to it in Romans 1:16, the gospel's power.

Passage #6 — Romans 6:1-14

In this particular section of Romans, Paul is responding to a supposed question about the efficiency of God's grace and one's attitude regarding God's mercy.

His answer indicates that the question seemed to be the following, "If God's grace ever expands to cover sin at every level of gravity, why not sin all the more in order to cause more of God's grace to be manifested?"

The question demonstrates a nice bit of sophistry (false argument) as well as a misunderstanding of how both sin and grace work in real life and not just a play on words in a religious debate.

> [1] What shall we say then? Are we to continue in sin so that grace may increase? [2] May it never be! How shall we who died to sin still live in it? [3] Or do you not know that all of us who have been baptized into Christ Jesus have been baptized into His death? [4] Therefore we have been buried with Him through baptism into death, so that as Christ was raised from the dead through the glory of the Father, so we too might walk in newness of life. [5] For if we have become united with Him in the likeness of His death, certainly we shall also be in the likeness of His resurrection, [6] knowing this, that our old self was crucified with Him, in order that our body of sin might be done away with, so that we would no longer be slaves to sin; [7] for he who has died is freed from sin.
> - Romans 6:1-7

First, Paul repeats and rejects the premise of the question (more sin producing more grace). In his reply, he points to the response believers make to the preaching of the gospel: repentance and baptism.

> Peter said to them, "Repent, and each of you be baptized in the name of Jesus Christ for the forgiveness of your sins; and you will receive the gift of the Holy Spirit.
> - Acts 2:38

Peter describes what those who believed in Jesus were to do in order to express their faith, Paul explains the meaning of what they were to do in response to the gospel.

The Judaizers, who insisted that conversion was not complete without circumcision, were attaching salvation to a symbol that tied a person to the people who carried the promise forward until the appearance of Jesus Christ who was sent to fulfill the promise. That symbol and ceremony (circumcision) was no longer necessary or relevant because the task it represented was complete (the task: a people faithfully carrying the promise forward until the Savior came, and circumcision being the symbol that one belonged to that covenant people).

Paul explains that the new symbol and ceremony, baptism (immersion in water), now expresses a more complete truth received and activated by faith. In baptism, we receive the blessings realized by the coming of the promise brought into this world by the Jewish people through the agency of the Holy Spirit. Paul explains that through baptism, a believer re-enacts the death, burial and resurrection of Jesus Christ. He points out, however, that our symbolic physical death, burial and resurrection in the waters of baptism has, not symbolic but actual spiritual results that circumcision only pointed to but could never accomplish.

The original problem that the promise of God was sent to fix was the issue of sin. Since Adam, all were guilty of sin and condemned to eternal separation from God because of it (Romans 3:23; Romans 6:23).

Even if man was aware of the effects of sin, he was helpless to avoid its consequences because his weakened spiritual nature could not overcome sin completely thus freeing him from its power, effect and consequences (Romans 3:9-12). Add to this mix the efforts of Satan to constantly lead the world into sinful behavior and thwart all sincere efforts to obey God and live righteously. The result was a world that knew what sin was and its consequences but helpless to eliminate or make restitution for it.

The good news that Paul preached and was explaining here was that Jesus offered His perfect sinless life through His death on the cross as a payment for the moral debt owed to God by sinful men and women. Once the debt was paid for and confirmed (i.e. the offering was acceptable to God: the resurrection – Romans 1:4), God now had a way to deal with sin that would bestow on imperfect people the gift and privilege of being united with Him once again. That manner, made possible by Jesus' cross, was a forgiveness received by faith, not a forgiveness produced by man's restitution... This was the GOOD NEWS!

Sins were forgiven in the waters of baptism because this is where the believing sinner expressed his faith in Jesus Christ.

1. Faith was not expressed in circumcision as the Judaizers argued.

2. Faith was not expressed in perfect obedience as the legalists and Pharisees claimed.

3. Faith was not expressed in the discovery of secret knowledge or loyalty to certain church leaders as the Gnostic teachers taught.

4. Faith was not expressed in severe treatment of the body, rejection of marriage and the making of vows as the ascetics then and now promote.

Since Pentecost Sunday when Peter preached the gospel for the first time after Jesus ascended into heaven, faith in Jesus Christ is the basis of our salvation which consists of:

1. Forgiveness for sins so that we can become acceptable and thus able to come before God.
2. We receive the indwelling of the Holy Spirit so we can live a faithful life in this world and after death be united with the Father and Jesus forever. The Holy Spirit joins with our spirit to enable these things (II Timothy 2:11-12a).

This section, among other things, was the teaching and response to every effort to change the gospel in any way. Paul explained what God's "promise," carried by the Jews, fulfilled and realized by Jesus and proclaimed by the Apostles, consisted of. He further taught how those who understood and believed the gospel were to respond, and described the very real blessings that those who responded faithfully would receive.

The second part of this section answers the question about sin and grace.

> [8]Now if we have died with Christ, we believe that we shall also live with Him, [9]knowing that Christ, having been raised from the dead, is never to die again; death no longer is master over Him. [10]For the death that He died, He died to sin once for all; but the life that He lives, He lives to God. [11]Even so consider yourselves to be dead to sin, but alive to God in Christ Jesus. [12]Therefore do not let sin reign in your mortal body so that you obey its lusts, [13]and do not go on presenting the members of your body to sin as instruments of unrighteousness; but present yourselves to God as those alive from the dead, and your members as instruments of righteousness to God. [14]For sin shall not be master over you, for you are not under law but under grace.
> - Romans 6:8-14

In this passage, Paul explains the true role of God's grace in a believer's life. Grace is not some kind of spiritual free pass that enables one to indulge in sin without guilt or consequences, as the question suggested.

In verse 14, Paul summarizes the entire passage by saying that we, Christians, are not under Law, meaning we are not judged by the Law (we are forgiven for all the offenses we committed in violation of the Law); in addition, we are not motivated or affected by the Law either. The purpose of the Law was to reveal sin and the punishment due for sin (Romans 3:19-20). As Christians we have been forgiven for all of our sins and consequently will not face condemnation nor punishment (Romans 8:1). This is how we are "not under Law."

Being under grace, on the other hand, meant that we are affected and empowered by grace.

A. Affected by grace

- It was God's grace that moved Him to make and send the promise (Romans 3:24).

- It was God's grace that offered salvation based on faith instead of Law (Ephesians 2:8-9).

- It is God's grace that moves God to bless us in this life with physical as well as all the blessings in the heavenly realm (Ephesians 1:3).

- It is God's grace that offers eternal life with Him and Jesus who sacrificed His life for us (Romans 5:21).

B. Empowered by grace

Unlike those who saw grace as something to be exploited for personal gratification, Paul explains that the opposite is true. God's grace exploits us to God's glory by enabling us to do the following:

1. Walk or live in a new way (vs. 4).

2. Break free from the grip or slavery to sin (vs. 6).

3. Be naturally drawn to God rather than naturally drawn to sin (vs. 11).

4. Willingly offer ourselves to God in worship and ministry (vs. 13).

5. Live in freedom, protected and motivated by God's grace rather than feeling guilty and dreading death and judgment (I Corinthians 15:9-10).

Summary

Throughout history, human misery has largely been caused by three lies from Satan.

Lie #1 – God is a liar. Believing this lie broke the union between man and God.

Lie #2 – Satan is God. This lie perpetuated man's focus on himself and what Satan controls in this world. This lie perpetuates the darkness wherever it is believed.

Lie #3 – Jesus is not God. Whether it is outright rejection of Jesus as God, or the undermining of His word, this lie is constantly mutating and altering its form and its source (e.g. sometimes atheist college professors, sometimes clergymen, sometimes politicians). The end goal is always the same, to deny Jesus His rightful position as the divine Son of God made man with all authority in heaven and on earth, and to discredit or change the promise made to mankind by God by altering His word or giving it a different meaning.

No matter how one summarizes the Bible (seven passages or seven hundred passages), the end result should always be the same. God the Father sent His divine Son to take on a human body in order to offer His life in death as a payment for the sins of mankind. Those who believe that Jesus is the Son of God and express their faith in repentance and baptism will be forgiven, they will receive the Holy Spirit and will have the guarantee of eternal life.

We should note that Satan's plan of attack is simple:

DESTROY THE MESSAGE = DESTROY THE CHURCH

PASSAGE #7
JOHN 17:1-3
THE PROMISE FULFILLED

Our study is based on the premise that in some future world where all digital information is processed, transmitted and stored by a joint business and government agency, the Bible becomes one of those books banned because its content includes material that is deemed subversive.

This means that Bibles are removed from the shelves of bookstores and digital copies are ordered deleted. Eventually no copies are left and all that remains is what people remember about the Bible. The challenge that would naturally arise in a situation such as this would be how to preserve and spread the core message of the Bible if no text was available.

Of course this is a story line one would find in a futuristic sci-fi drama, but just for argument's sake, "How would believers preserve and pass on the message of the Bible if this situation came to pass?" One suggestion, detailed in this book, would be to select a number of passages that summarized the key ideas and teachings of the Bible which then could easily be memorized, shared and passed on in order to keep the gospel message alive. This method would be much like the "oral histories" passed down from generation to generation in ancient times before writing and printed materials were widely used.

"The Bible in Seven Passages," therefore, is an attempt to identify seven key passages that actually contain enough information to summarize the entire 66 books that make up the holy Bible.

Seven Passages – Review

1. **Genesis 1:1 – Prelude to the promise: creation** – Genesis 1:1 is the foundational verse in the Bible because it not only explains how the world came into being, but who created it.

2. **Genesis 3:1-24 – God's promise to fallen man** – This passage explains how man and the creation came to be in their present fallen and imperfect condition, and introduces a promise of redemption in the future.

3. **Genesis 11:27 – 12:7 – The person of promise: historical** – God's promise is given a human identity that can be traced through the history of the Jewish people.

4. **Isaiah 53:1-12 – The person of promise: spiritual** – God's promise is identified through prophecy, which describes the person and mission of the promise from a spiritual perspective.

5. **John 3:14-16 – The promise revealed** – The details of the promise are clearly revealed and explained.

6. **Romans 6:1-14 – The promise realized** – Paul explains how the promise is realized in a person's life here on earth through the effects of grace on those who receive the promise through faith.

7. **John 17:1-3 – The promise fulfilled** – The seventh passage describes the final state of all who believe and

remain faithful to the promise as they pass from the earthly to the eternal heavenly realm.

Passage #7

> [1] Jesus spoke these things; and lifting up His eyes to heaven, He said, "Father, the hour has come; glorify Your Son, that the Son may glorify You, [2] even as You gave Him authority over all flesh, that to all whom You have given Him, He may give eternal life. [3] This is eternal life, that they may know You, the only true God, and Jesus Christ whom You have sent.
> - John 17:1-3

Jesus spoke these words as part of the teaching, encouragement and prayer he offered up after sharing the Passover meal with His Apostles and just before His arrest leading up to His death by crucifixion.

In this passage, Jesus refers to the suffering, death and resurrection He will experience in the days to come. He also includes the "glory" the Father will give Him by confirming His exalted status as the divine Son of God (by resurrecting Him from the dead) – a point that is also made by Paul the Apostle in Romans 1:4.

Jesus also states, in simple terms, the essence of the promise which had been made by God in the garden; carried forward throughout history by the Jewish nation; confirmed and articulated by the prophets; and now about to be realized through His atoning death on the cross and proof of attainment for all who believed through His glorious resurrection.

Jesus signals to all believers that God's promise of eternal life was about to be made possible, and the proof that He could deliver on this promise was His own resurrection from a sure and terrible death on the cross.

This promise and its subsequent fulfillment in His own resurrection was enough to provide hope and joy to all of His followers. Jesus, however, goes one step further by describing the nature of this experience referred to as "eternal life."

Jesus not only reveals that believers will consciously exist after they die, He also describes what this existence will be like! Not just "how long" we will live (forever) but "how" that experience of life will be!

Eternal Life

> This is eternal life, that they may know You, the only true God, and Jesus Christ whom You have sent.
> - John 17:3

The essence of eternal life is the experience of knowledge, and this experience continuing without end. The believer, because of and through the agency of the Holy Spirit, will experience the filling of his being with knowledge. The original Greek word translated into the English word "know" in this passage means the intimate knowing of another with understanding, with appreciation, enlightenment and awareness. This is how we will know the true and living God (the Father) as well as have the same knowledge of God the Son (Jesus).

This will be possible because of two reasons:

1. We will possess a glorified body after our own resurrection from the dead.

> [42]So also is the resurrection of the dead. It is sown a perishable body, it is raised an imperishable body; [43]it is

> sown in dishonor, it is raised in glory; it is sown in weakness, it is raised in power; [44]it is sown a natural body, it is raised a spiritual body. If there is a natural body, there is also a spiritual body. [45]So also it is written, "The first MAN, Adam, BECAME A LIVING SOUL." The last Adam became a life-giving spirit. [46]However, the spiritual is not first, but the natural; then the spiritual. [47]The first man is from the earth, earthy; the second man is from heaven. [48]As is the earthy, so also are those who are earthy; and as is the heavenly, so also are those who are heavenly. [49]Just as we have borne the image of the earthy, we will also bear the image of the heavenly.
> - I Corinthians 15:42-49

This body will enable us to be in the presence of God without harm since the glorified body will not be subject to sin or death.

2. The Holy Spirit will enable our own spirit to interact with God.

The Holy Spirit helped us to overcome sin, to live according to God's will and to offer acceptable prayers to God (Romans 8:13; 14; 27), when we had physical bodies. The same Holy Spirit will enable resurrected believers to experience the never-ending growth of the knowledge of God and Christ that is referred to as eternal life.

Every religion has an afterlife scenario. Atheism and other philosophies that try to explain life without reference to God teach that there is no life or consciousness after death. Hinduism and other eastern religions say that individual consciousness merges with a higher "force" and thus ceases to be. Other monotheistic religions see the afterlife as a perfected version of life on earth where physical and emotional appetites are satisfied. Biblical Christianity teaches that life after death is primarily focused on a heightened understanding and knowledge of the Godhead of which, through Christ, believers have become a part. This means that:

A. Believers will have a relationship with God based on knowledge and appreciation, not sin and death.

Sin and death are part of the physical world which will have passed away in judgment, destruction and memory. Believers will live in the perpetual now and will no longer experience the yesterday, today and tomorrow context that measured their physical existence. Eternal life consists of an ever growing and dynamic relationship between God and believers within the Godhead in the eternal now.

B. Eternal life will be based on unfettered adoration and not service.

Service was necessary in the physical world because of the various needs that arose on account of sin. Christians served the needs of others (even the need to evangelize) because in doing so were fulfilling God's command to love and serve others in the name of Christ. There are no "needs" in the Godhead, but there will always be the natural impetus for the created to worship the Creator. This worship will no longer be impeded by human weakness, ignorance or sin. Eternal life will permit worship that is in spirit and truth because it will be enhanced and informed by ever increasing knowledge and understanding of the object of worship: the true and living God.

C. Eternal life will be an existence not only anticipated, but fully realized and experienced.

The Christian believer begins to experience the eternal life that he anticipates after death in the present life. Unlike many other religions where the afterlife reward is only received after death, the Christian begins to experience his afterlife reward in this present life. For example, the follower of Jesus is promised the joy of a sinless existence in heaven but actually begins to taste what that is like when he becomes a Christian by expressing his faith in Jesus through repentance and baptism (Acts 2:37-38). According to this and many other verses in the New Testament (e.g. Acts 22:16) sins are actually forgiven at baptism because God has provided an atoning sacrifice to remove them (Isaiah 53:5; I Peter 2:21-25).

The Christian, therefore, receives actual forgiveness now and experiences the corresponding relief, joy, gratitude and peace in this world because his sins are forgiven now, not only in the future. His eternal life is guaranteed now even before he goes to the next world. The knowing of God (and the rewards of this knowledge) is possible in this life but will be fully realized when all the obstacles to this end that exist in this world are removed in the next.

D. We will exist within the Godhead, not apart from it – I Corinthians 15:28.

Jesus' ultimate mission was to bring man into the Godhead.

> If we endure, we will also reign with Him;
> If we deny Him, He also will deny us;
> - II Timothy 2:12

Jesus changed the composition of His divine nature to include a human nature. He did not discard or change back His nature to eliminate this altered state after he ascended to heaven. Note that He appeared to the Apostles and ascended back into heaven in His altered nature as Jesus – the God/man.

Our faith in God and our belief in Jesus will grant us an eternal life which will allow us to forever know and experience the things only God knows and experiences. In a word, this ultimate knowledge and experience is perfect, eternal love. We know that this is the nature of the knowledge and understanding that eternal life within the Godhead will bring believers to because John tells us that this is the essence of God's being.

> ⁷Beloved, let us love one another, for love is from God; and everyone who loves is born of God and knows God. ⁸The one who does not love does not know God, for God is love. ⁹By this the love of God was manifested in us, that God has sent His only begotten Son into the world so that we might live through Him. ¹⁰In this is love, not that we loved God, but that He loved us and sent His Son to be the propitiation for our sins. ¹¹Beloved, if God so loved us, we also ought to love one another. ¹²No one has seen God at any time; if we love one another, God abides in us, and His love is perfected in us. ¹³By this we know that we abide in Him and He in us, because He has given us of His Spirit. ¹⁴We have seen and testify that the Father has sent the Son to be the Savior of the world.
> - I John 4:7-14

Note that love is the touchstone for everything done by God to give believers eternal life. Love was the basis from which the promise was made, sent and completed. Love is also the basis for the realization and fulfillment of the promise. Love from the beginning to the everlasting end. This is why all sin is, in fact, violence against love in one way or another.

Hell, therefore, is existence without love, which ultimately is no existence at all since existence cannot be sustained without a measure of love. Therefore, hell does exist but those there cannot be sustained forever and in this is seen the judgment and mercy of God in that those who go to hell go to a real dimension of mind and sense and suffering, but cannot survive there.

Mankind's end, therefore, is either intimate loving knowledge of God within the Godhead forever or the separation from God into nothingness forever.

Summary

Let's hope that God will spare us the type of future I have talked about in this series. A future where access to the Bible is denied or restricted. A future where we would be forced to carry an abbreviated form of it just to summarize its message and pass it on to others. (I am not sure this could be done, considering our laws, but there are many who would like to see it done.)

If, however, this did happen, here once again are the seven passages I would choose to summarize the Bible:

Passage #1 - Genesis 1:1

> In the beginning God created the heavens and the earth.

Passage #2 - Genesis 3:1-24

> ¹Now the serpent was more crafty than any beast of the field which the LORD God had made. And he said to the woman, "Indeed, has God said, 'You shall not eat from any tree of the garden'?" ²The woman said to the serpent, "From the fruit of the trees of the garden we may eat; ³but from the fruit of the tree which is in the middle of the garden, God has said, 'You shall not eat from it or touch it, or you will die.'" ⁴The serpent said to the woman, "You surely will not die! ⁵For God knows that in the day you eat from it your eyes will be opened, and you will be like God, knowing good and evil." ⁶When the woman saw that the tree was good for food, and that it was a delight to the eyes, and that the tree was desirable to make one wise, she took from its fruit and ate; and she gave also to her husband with her, and he ate. ⁷Then the eyes of both of them were opened, and they knew that they were naked; and they sewed fig leaves together and made themselves loin

coverings.
⁸They heard the sound of the LORD God walking in the garden in the cool of the day, and the man and his wife hid themselves from the presence of the LORD God among the trees of the garden. ⁹Then the LORD God called to the man, and said to him, "Where are you?" ¹⁰He said, "I heard the sound of You in the garden, and I was afraid because I was naked; so I hid myself." ¹¹And He said, "Who told you that you were naked? Have you eaten from the tree of which I commanded you not to eat?" ¹²The man said, "The woman whom You gave to be with me, she gave me from the tree, and I ate." ¹³Then the LORD God said to the woman, "What is this you have done?" And the woman said, "The serpent deceived me, and I ate." ¹⁴The LORD God said to the serpent,
"Because you have done this,
Cursed are you more than all cattle,
And more than every beast of the field;
On your belly you will go,
And dust you will eat
All the days of your life;
¹⁵And I will put enmity
Between you and the woman,
And between your seed and her seed;
He shall bruise you on the head,
And you shall bruise him on the heel."
¹⁶To the woman He said,
"I will greatly multiply
Your pain in childbirth,
In pain you will bring forth children;
Yet your desire will be for your husband,
And he will rule over you."
¹⁷Then to Adam He said, "Because you have listened to the voice of your wife, and have eaten from the tree about which I commanded you, saying, 'You shall not eat from it';
Cursed is the ground because of you;
In toil you will eat of it

All the days of your life.
¹⁸"Both thorns and thistles it shall grow for you;
And you will eat the plants of the field;
¹⁹By the sweat of your face
You will eat bread,
Till you return to the ground,
Because from it you were taken;
For you are dust,
And to dust you shall return."
²⁰Now the man called his wife's name Eve, because she was the mother of all the living. ²¹The LORD God made garments of skin for Adam and his wife, and clothed them.
²²Then the LORD God said, "Behold, the man has become like one of Us, knowing good and evil; and now, he might stretch out his hand, and take also from the tree of life, and eat, and live forever"— ²³therefore the LORD God sent him out from the garden of Eden, to cultivate the ground from which he was taken. ²⁴So He drove the man out; and at the east of the garden of Eden He stationed the cherubim and the flaming sword which turned every direction to guard the way to the tree of life.

Passage #3 - Genesis 11:27 – 12:7

²⁷Now these are the records of the generations of Terah. Terah became the father of Abram, Nahor and Haran; and Haran became the father of Lot. ²⁸Haran died in the presence of his father Terah in the land of his birth, in Ur of the Chaldeans. ²⁹Abram and Nahor took wives for themselves. The name of Abram's wife was Sarai; and the name of Nahor's wife was Milcah, the daughter of Haran, the father of Milcah and Iscah. ³⁰Sarai was barren; she had no child.
³¹Terah took Abram his son, and Lot the son of Haran, his grandson, and Sarai his daughter-in-law, his son Abram's wife; and they went out together from Ur of

the Chaldeans in order to enter the land of Canaan; and they went as far as Haran, and settled there. ³²The days of Terah were two hundred and five years; and Terah died in Haran.

¹Now the LORD said to Abram,
"[Go forth from your country,
And from your relatives
And from your father's house,
To the land which I will show you;
²And I will make you a great nation,
And I will bless you,
And make your name great;
And so you shall be a blessing;
³And I will bless those who bless you,
And the one who curses you I will curse.
And in you all the families of the earth will be blessed."
⁴So Abram went forth as the LORD had spoken to him; and Lot went with him. Now Abram was seventy-five years old when he departed from Haran. ⁵Abram took Sarai his wife and Lot his nephew, and all their possessions which they had accumulated, and the persons which they had acquired in Haran, and they set out for the land of Canaan; thus they came to the land of Canaan. ⁶Abram passed through the land as far as the site of Shechem, to the oak of Moreh. Now the Canaanite was then in the land. ⁷The LORD appeared to Abram and said, "To your descendants I will give this land." So he built an altar there to the LORD who had appeared to him.

Passage #4 - Isaiah 53:1-12

¹Who has believed our message?
And to whom has the arm of the LORD been revealed?
²For He grew up before Him like a tender shoot,
And like a root out of parched ground;
He has no stately form or majesty
That we should look upon Him,

Nor appearance that we should be attracted to Him.
³He was despised and forsaken of men,
A man of sorrows and acquainted with grief;
And like one from whom men hide their face
He was despised, and we did not esteem Him.
⁴Surely our griefs He Himself bore,
And our sorrows He carried;
Yet we ourselves esteemed Him stricken,
Smitten of God, and afflicted.
⁵But He was pierced through for our transgressions,
He was crushed for our iniquities;
The chastening for our well-being fell upon Him,
And by His scourging we are healed.
⁶All of us like sheep have gone astray,
Each of us has turned to his own way;
But the LORD has caused the iniquity of us all
To fall on Him.
⁷He was oppressed and He was afflicted,
Yet He did not open His mouth;
Like a lamb that is led to slaughter,
And like a sheep that is silent before its shearers,
So He did not open His mouth.
⁸By oppression and judgment He was taken away;
And as for His generation, who considered
That He was cut off out of the land of the living
For the transgression of my people, to whom the stroke was due?
⁹His grave was assigned with wicked men,
Yet He was with a rich man in His death,
Because He had done no violence,
Nor was there any deceit in His mouth.
¹⁰But the LORD was pleased
To crush Him, putting Him to grief;
If He would render Himself as a guilt offering,
He will see His offspring,
He will prolong His days,
And the good pleasure of the LORD will prosper in His hand.
¹¹As a result of the anguish of His soul,

> He will see it and be satisfied;
> By His knowledge the Righteous One,
> My Servant, will justify the many,
> As He will bear their iniquities.
> ¹²Therefore, I will allot Him a portion with the great,
> And He will divide the booty with the strong;
> Because He poured out Himself to death,
> And was numbered with the transgressors;
> Yet He Himself bore the sin of many,
> And interceded for the transgressors.

Passage #5 - John 3:14-16

> ¹⁴As Moses lifted up the serpent in the wilderness, even so must the Son of Man be lifted up; ¹⁵so that whoever believes will in Him have eternal life. ¹⁶"For God so loved the world, that He gave His only begotten Son, that whoever believes in Him shall not perish, but have eternal life.

Passage #6 - Romans 6:1-14

> ¹What shall we say then? Are we to continue in sin so that grace may increase? ²May it never be! How shall we who died to sin still live in it? ³Or do you not know that all of us who have been baptized into Christ Jesus have been baptized into His death? ⁴Therefore we have been buried with Him through baptism into death, so that as Christ was raised from the dead through the glory of the Father, so we too might walk in newness of life. ⁵For if we have become united with Him in the likeness of His death, certainly we shall also be in the likeness of His resurrection, ⁶knowing this, that our old self was crucified with Him, in order that our body of sin might be done away with, so that we would no longer be slaves to sin; ⁷for he who has died is freed from sin.

> [8]Now if we have died with Christ, we believe that we shall also live with Him, [9]knowing that Christ, having been raised from the dead, is never to die again; death no longer is master over Him. [10]For the death that He died, He died to sin once for all; but the life that He lives, He lives to God. [11]Even so consider yourselves to be dead to sin, but alive to God in Christ Jesus. [12]Therefore do not let sin reign in your mortal body so that you obey its lusts, [13]and do not go on presenting the members of your body to sin as instruments of unrighteousness; but present yourselves to God as those alive from the dead, and your members as instruments of righteousness to God. [14]For sin shall not be master over you, for you are not under law but under grace.

Passage #7 - John 17:1-3

> [1]Jesus spoke these things; and lifting up His eyes to heaven, He said, "Father, the hour has come; glorify Your Son, that the Son may glorify You, [2]even as You gave Him authority over all flesh, that to all whom You have given Him, He may give eternal life. [3]This is eternal life, that they may know You, the only true God, and Jesus Christ whom You have sent.

In closing, let me suggest that a good exercise of study would be to find your own seven passages to summarize the Bible.

BibleTalk.tv is an Internet Mission Work.

We provide textual Bible teaching material on our website and mobile apps for free. We enable churches and individuals all over the world to have access to high-quality Bible materials for personal growth, group study or for teaching in their classes.

The goal of this mission work is to spread the gospel to the greatest number of people using the latest technology available. For the first time in history it is becoming possible to preach the gospel to the entire world at once. BibleTalk.tv is an effort to preach the gospel to all nations every day until Jesus returns.

The Choctaw Church of Christ in Oklahoma City is the sponsoring congregation for this work and provides the oversight for the BibleTalk.tv ministry team. If you would like information on how you can support this ministry, please go to the link provided below.

---

bibletalk.tv/support

Made in the USA
San Bernardino, CA
23 January 2020